Machines at Work

★ A very first picture book ★

The original publishers would like to thank the following children (and their parents) for appearing in this book: Milo Clare, Jamie Grant, Bella Haycraft Mee, Lily Haycraft Mee, Jasmine Haynes, Joseph Haynes, Rhys Hillier, Rebekah Murrell, and Chanelle Robinson.

For a free color catalog describing Gareth Stevens Publishing's list of high-quality books and multimedia programs, call 1-800-542-2595 (USA) or 1-800-461-9120 (Canada). Gareth Stevens Publishing's Fax: (414) 225-0377.

Library of Congress Cataloging-in-Publication Data

Tuxworth, Nicola.
    Machines at work: a very first picture book / Nicola Tuxworth.
      p. cm. — (Pictures and words)
    Includes bibliographical references and index.
    Summary: Simple text and photographs of children playing with toys present such useful vehicles as the tractor, dump truck, and fire engine.
    ISBN 0-8368-2432-6 (lib. bdg.)
    1. Machinery—Juvenile literature. [1. Vehicles.] I. Title. II. Series.
TJ147.T89   1999
621.8—dc21   99-19213

This North American edition first published in 1999 by
Gareth Stevens Publishing
1555 North RiverCenter Drive, Suite 201
Milwaukee, WI 53212 USA

Original edition © 1997 by Anness Publishing Limited. First published in 1997 by Lorenz Books, an imprint of Anness Publishing Inc., New York, New York. This U.S. edition © 1999 by Gareth Stevens, Inc. Additional end matter © 1999 by Gareth Stevens, Inc.

Senior editor: Sue Grabham
Photographer: Lucy Tizard
Stylist: Isolde Sommerfeldt
Assistant stylist: Jenny Catherine Freeman
Design and typesetting: Michael Leaman Design Partnership

Printed in Mexico

1 2 3 4 5 6 7 8 9 03 02 01 00 99

Machines at Work

★ A very first picture book ★

Nicola Tuxworth

Gareth Stevens Publishing
MILWAUKEE

Cranes can lift objects
high in the air.

I need to
move these
bricks.

4

Up it goes!
Wheeee!

crane

5

Tractors carry food
for all the animals
on the farm.

Fill the truck
with hay...

6

...and off we go.
Vroom! Vroom!

tractor

Dump trucks carry heavy
loads across building sites.

Fill the truck
with gravel...

...and dump
it in a pile.
Whoosh!

dump
truck

This machine mixes cement.

Turn the handle
to mix in the sand...

...and out
comes the
cement.
Splat!

...ment
...xer

11

Garbage trucks are used
to collect the trash.

There is
room for
some more
trash...

cen
mi

...so I will
dump it in.
Crash!

garbage
truck

13

Fire engines carry firefighters,
ladders, and hoses to fires.

I have to
put out a fire!

Almost there!
Wooo! Wooo!

fire engine

Backhoes dig up
dirt and sand.

Scoop up
the sand...

...and dump
it over here.
Rrrrroar!

backhoe

17

Tow trucks rescue cars and their passengers.

Has your car broken down?

18

I'll tow you
to the garage.
Clankety clank!

tow truck

A bulldozer can push very heavy loads with its strong blade.

Fill up
the blade...

...and drop
the bricks.
Crash! Bang! Smash!

bulldozer

When I grow up, I want
to be a firefighter!

Questions for Discussion

1. Besides bricks, what can a crane lift into the air? Where might you go to see a crane at work?

2. What equipment do firefighters carry with them on the fire truck?

3. Can you think of any other kinds of trucks, besides the ones shown in this book?

4. What kinds of things do you need to learn to be a good crane operator? A good truck driver? A good firefighter?

5. Compare the trucks in this book. Which trucks have four wheels? Which trucks have more than four wheels? How are all the trucks alike? How are they different?

More Books to Read

Barney's Book of Trucks.
   Monica Mody
   (Lyrick Publishing)

The Big Book of Things That Go.
   Caroline Bingham
   (Dorling Kindersley)

Big Machines: Trucks.
   Jan Pienkowski
   (Dutton)

Big Rigs.
   Hope Irvin Marston
   (Cobblehill Books)

Construction.
   Gallimard Jeunesse
   and Philippe Biard
   (Scholastic)

Construction Zone.
   Tana Hoban
   (Greenwillow Books)

Videos

Fire and Rescue.
(Fred Levine Productions)

Movin' Dirt. (Child Like
Productions)

Road Construction Ahead.
(Fred Levine Productions)

There Goes a Bulldozer.
(Kid Vision)

Web Sites

ftpl.rad.kumc.edu/clips/vehi
cles/trucks/index.htm

www.komatsu.co.ip/kikki/zu
kan/e-index.htm

Some web sites stay current longer than others. For further web sites, use your search engines to locate the following topics: *bulldozers, cement mixers, construction, fire trucks, tractors,* and *trucks.*

Glossary-Index

collect: to bring objects together. (p. 12)

crane: a large machine with a swinging arm that lifts and carries heavy objects. (pp. 4-5)

gravel: a loose mixture of small stones or pieces of rock. (p. 8)

hay: dried grass and other plants. (p. 6)

heavy: weighing a lot. (pp. 8, 20)

rescue: to save something or someone from danger or harm. (p. 18)

tow: to pull something along behind with a rope or chain, like a car being pulled behind a tow truck. (pp. 18-19)

24